AUNT KELLY IS A REALTOR

Anita Rowe Stafford

Published by Laughing Ladybug Press

AUNT KELLY IS A REALTOR

First edition. May 26, 2022.

Written by Anita Rowe Stafford.

Aunt Kelly is a realtor. She lives in St. Louis, Missouri, with her husband and two children. Her job is to help people when they want to buy or sell a house.

Aunt Kelly first became interested in becoming a realtor several years ago when her own house was for sale. She needed a realtor's help, and she saw how important it is to give good customer service. After her experience, she decided she would like to be a realtor.

Aunt Kelly then took classes to learn all the skills she needed and to obtain a license to sell real estate. When she finished her studies she went to work in a real estate office with other realtors.

Now many different kinds of families come to Aunt Kelly for help with buying or selling their houses. Aunt Kelly starts by asking questions to find out how she can help.

Sometimes people have a large house they want to sell. After their children have grown up, a big house might be too difficult for older people to care for.

Aunt Kelly helps them sell their large house and find a smaller house that is perfect for them.

When families come to Aunt Kelly for help with buying a house, she knows that moving is not always easy for the children. It can be a happy experience, but sometimes it can be sad or scary, too. Aunt Kelly says it can make the move easier if children are allowed to choose the color of their new bedroom. She also says kids adjust better when familiar items, such as bedding, are used in the new house.

The questions asked by Aunt Kelly help her to know what's important to each family. Are they looking for a house or a condominium? How many bedrooms do they need? Do they want a house with stairs or no stairs? How much money do they want to invest in their house? What school do they want to be near?

SCHOOL
SCHOOL

Some families are made up of people from different generations. Grandparents, parents, and children may live together and care for each other. Aunt Kelly asks questions to find out what the family needs to make all the generations comfortable.

Every family is special in its own way. Some families need a house with ramps instead of steps at the entrance. Other families want to be sure the yard is fenced to keep their pets safe.

When people are looking for a house to buy, some of them want a new, modern house in a nice suburban neighborhood.

Other people want a smaller house far out in the country. Aunt Kelly helps families find a house in the location that is right for them.

When a family wants to build a house, Aunt Kelly helps find a building lot for them.

Aunt Kelly might help them plan and design their new house. She can also help them find the right builder.

Some people come to Aunt Kelly looking for fixer-upper houses to buy. They don't want to buy a house to live in, instead, they want to buy a house that needs repairs. Usually houses like this can be bought at a lower price, then the buyer will fix it up like new and re-sell it.

When a family wants to buy a house to live in, an inspection is done to be sure everything about the house is in good working order. If the seller needs to make repairs, Aunt Kelly will help them find the right workers.

Painting is one of the easiest ways to improve the appearance of a house. A painter can make the walls look clean and new again.

A plumber can replace old, worn out fixtures or pipes that leak.

Some houses need new wiring or new lighting. Aunt Kelly can help find an electrician to do the job.

Aunt Kelly often works with banks and title companies for her clients. Most families need to borrow some money when they buy a house. An important part of a realtor's job is to help people find a place to borrow the money they need. She also helps them read and understand contracts to be sure their home and money are protected.

It's a very happy day for a realtor like Aunt Kelly when a sale is closed. On closing day the buyers receive keys to their new property. Usually by this time, Aunt Kelly has made new friends because she has spent so much time working with the buyers or the sellers.

Aunt Kelly knows she has done her job well when she helps a family find and buy their dream home.

Now that you know about Aunt Kelly and her work, it's time to think about what kind of work you might do when you grow up. Maybe you'll want to do the same kind of work your parents do. Or maybe you'll decide you want to be a realtor like Aunt Kelly.

Also by Anita Stafford

Picture books
A Vegetable Garden is Not For Cows
Briley Isabelle Gordon Wants a Cat
The Disappearance of Mr. White
Vegetables Smegetables
Hooray Hooray It's Purple Day
We Are Different, We Are the Same
Laughing Ladybug Meets the Grumpy Bugs
If Moms Were Flowers I'd Pick You
Can You See Me Now: Cheetahs Hiding in Plain Sight
The Squirrel School Picnic

The Career Kids Series
Uncle Philip is a Farmer
Aunt Tiffany is an Artist
Aunt Virginia is a Seamstress

Chapter books
The Sassafras House series including:
The Legend of Sassafras House
Treasure in Catclaw Canyon
The Catnapper Mystery

For adults
Confessions of a Cell Phone Loser

Watch for more at www.anitastafford.com

About the Author

Anita Rowe Stafford makes her home in northeastern Arkansas. She worked in public school for more than twenty years as a teacher and a counselor. Anita has taught students from kindergarten to graduate level, and she is also a Licensed Professional Counselor.